ENGRAVED

SNOWBOUND SERIES CHAPBOOK AWARD WINNERS

Barbara Tran, *In the Mynah Bird's Own Words*
Selected by Robert Wrigley

David Hernandez, *A House Waiting for Music*
Selected by Ray Gonzalez

Mark Yakich, *The Making of Collateral Beauty*
Selected by Mary Ruefle

Joy Katz, *The Garden Room*
Selected by Lisa Russ Spaar

Cecilia Woloch, *Narcissus*
Selected by Marie Howe

John Cross, *staring at the animal*
Selected by Gillian Conoley

Stacey Waite, *the lake has no saint*
Selected by Dana Levin

Brandon Som, *Babel's Moon*
Selected by Aimee Nezhukumatathil

Kathleen Jesme, *Meridian*
Selected by Patricia Fargnoli

Anna George Meek, *Engraved*
Selected by Ellen Doré Watson

EN GRA VED

POEMS

ANNA GEORGE MEEK

Tupelo Press
NORTH ADAMS, MASSACHUSETTS

Engraved.
Copyright 2013 Anna George Meek. All rights reserved.
ISBN: 978-1-936797-37-0

Cover and text design by Howard Klein.
Cover art from The Devil's Artisan (http://devilsartisan.ca).

First paperback edition: September, 2013.

No part of this book may be reproduced by any means without permission of the publisher. Please address permissions requests to:
Tupelo Press
P.O. Box 1767, North Adams, Massachusetts 01247
Telephone: (413) 664-9611
editor@tupelopress.org / www.tupelopress.org

Tupelo Press is an award-winning independent literary press that publishes fine poetry, fiction, and nonfiction in books that are a joy to hold as well as read. Tupelo Press is a registered 501(c)3 nonprofit organization, and we rely on public support to carry out our mission of publishing extraordinary work that may be outside the realm of the large commercial publishers. Financial donations are welcome and are tax deductible.

For anyone who has laid down lines and vanished from the earth.

And for my father (1937–2007).

CONTENTS

Imagine the Engraver	3
Cephalata	4
Pediculina Louse (On Human Hair)	6
Ribcage	7
Segment of a Circle	9
Teeth of Man	10
Fibrous	11
Spurs of Planets	13
Gargoyle/Gargoyle	14
Harlequin Duck	15
Map	17
Vampire (True Vampire), Vampire (False Vampire)	18
Vision	19
Toboggan Slide, with Toboggans, & Persons in Toboggan Suits	20
Vocal Organs in Vowel Positions	21
Acknowledgments	24

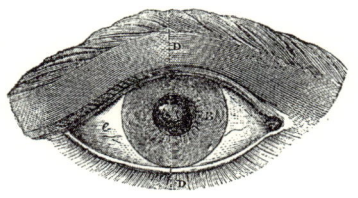

From 1859 to 1909, G. & C. Merriam Company employed artisans—many of whose names have been lost—to engrave images for the Merriam-Webster's Dictionary, the first illustrated dictionary in the United States.

ENGRAVED

IMAGINE THE ENGRAVER

By gaslight, the engraver's knife
carves Bayonet, Steam Engine, Mango
Tree. The mind in his century

grows warm near Cupola Furnace
as he defines his world imaginary, microscopic,
or extinct. Griffins, Hellbender, Deathwatch fly;
a Frigate sails in his soft wood block;
the seas burgeon with all manner of fish.

For a while, I live
in the images. New York Harbor
clutters with masts. Boiler, shiny,
opens its chambers

numbered in a fanciful hand. Every idea seen!
He clothes the naked words with Fez, Corset,
or Submarine Armor.

For the word Leviathan,
he carves a dictionary.

Every idea seen except

Engraver. Kin to me—I am trying to see
how. Sun & Planet Wheels, Buddha,
Bridge of Sighs, Passenger

Pigeon. These lines, a love letter to the dead.
Atlas bends his head.
Saturn Devours His Son.

CEPHALATA

Creature, knobby-headed, tilts
    downward; each tentacle

curls and thrusts in the blank, undrawn sea.
    In this word, the brain

is also an octopus. It swims
    where the light

cannot touch. No one sees the mythical
    rippling; it plunges

blind. It folds and releases and folds
    thought into

muscled morsels, tenses and
    consumes. I lose myself

in its rubbery webbing. The octopus
    and I are still

separate ideas. But words
    change

shape: *encephalitis,* and the brain
    inflames, sickness,

loss; the octopus struggles.
    Even enfolded, I

am supple; conscious effort; think
    of love and music

and raw fish, no not raw fish—*music,*
> music to become

my own creature, identifiable, joyful.
> It is possible to love

that which has utterly disappeared.
> Pitch the mind

what loves the pull of grief in black water.

PEDICULINA LOUSE (ON HUMAN HAIR)

Paisley design, teardrop with a thousand
little legs, lovely
creature, perched

in the illustration with her nits
upon thick cables. The heads of the unwashed
buzz with beauty. I imagine the Pediculina

crawls up the page to Peacock,
and its showier tail; the Pediculina pauses,

takes a left to Passenger
Pigeon. From there, the Pendulant Heart

looks like a wasp's nest.
Off the page, at a hospital

cafeteria, one woman turns over
another random thought

of her recently
dead father, the writer. How he fanned

his beautiful proud feathers. Her mind
wanders: diving bell, sperm whale,
terminal bud, whipworm. Back

to her father, image so detailed and lifelike,
the odd feeling makes her
scalp

prickle.

RIBCAGE

a) 1st Vertebra;
> see here etched where my breath caught.
> This is a diagram of surprise, or fear, and all
> around the block print, darkness. Beyond
> the ribcage, the universe unknown.

b) Sternum;
> where I love thee, no matter whom. I am
> merely illustrating one possibility.

c) Clavicle;
> the bones play music upon the clavichord,
> hold the melodies up in the same manner
> a coat hanger drapes translucent fabric.
> How the ivories themselves are bone,
> tusks, ribs of music. Nocturnes hang upon
> slim frames, and the light shines vaguely
> through.

d) Sternal Cartilages;
> which will be eaten when I am buried.
> After which, they must be supposed or
> imagined. None of this is real, though it is
> a facsimile of truth. I offer this as testimony of what had been.

e) 12th vertebra;
> believe all this or not, as faith guides thee;

in the beginning, *someone* imagined the word. ~~And now forgotten, how each carved line held import; cutting across the lines was regarded with horror.~~

f) Scapula;
> formerly, wings.

g), h), i) Ribs (Sternal, Asternal, Floating);
> like a great masted ship, so that we might breathe, its ribs pushing and pushing away an ocean rushing in.

SEGMENT OF A CIRCLE

Like a Cheshire cat, the circle does not
show itself, save for this one
raised eyebrow. O circle,
we imagine thee. Centuries
are round, and they disappear
beyond the curve of the earth.
The engraver is long dead; even I
am only partially visible. Believer
or skeptic, I can only have faith
that the moon appears behind me
when I turn away, can only
dream of its light, the universe, and
all gibbous time, shining entire.

TEETH OF MAN

See, the engraver has pulled them
from the jaw, sets them out
in order as if to string on a necklace.
Their roots reach up like claws,
and they will clutch there long
after flesh. A century later,
will you know me by my teeth?

Dearest,
bring me a teacup, says the gentleman
to his wasp-waisted woman. In lust,
his lip trembles against the lower
bicuspids, as ivory as an ascot.
Their sick child dreaming,
her big push out her small.
She mumbles in her sleep, images
in her head. *Enunciate, Sweet Thing,*
her father whispers, wanting
to understand. But her teeth
are loose. There is a gap.

I am grinding the gristle
to clarity—such the instinct to carve.
Even the queen masticates.
The enamel, we call it the crown;
but then, the canines.

FIBROUS

Illustrated like   a bare tree in winter:
small image, outline only, the word   bears
                      branches.
                      Or seen from above,

    rivers flowing into a vital artery. Then out to sea,

where a whaling vessel is   blown off course
by the storm, and the men
                adrift and salty with thirst,
        have no lines about them

    but madness. Then one day I grow mad
like my father.

        The memory that grew here first,

        where   does it start or end, and
        what did it look like?   Pointy, small,
                      described

    by one simple angled line. An idea books

passage,   the mind sails   the narrow channels

only to wreck on uncharted land. Our fibrous

family tree sends   tendrils and
    tangles
among my neurons,   like invasive ivy

    driving native species to   extinction.
                        In the logs
        of the old schooner's ruin:

                "Private Adam found a large beaked bird
                with no wings, large enough
                to give meat to our entire crew."

                      Afterward the men—
all lost.

SPURS OF PLANETS

The planets extend long tentacles,
claws on the ends of each, reach

cautiously for another orb,
and Earth a muscled thing.

No stars; the spheres whorl in modesty;
the universe blushes black.

In this cosmos, one might have drawn love
or defined it fearful

as creatures of the deep, with suckers
and no eyes. Spinning

to the outer reaches, an asteroid:
strange object sketched

in observers' journals at the edge
of understanding.

The heavens are grotesque,
or perhaps are we.

GARGOYLE / GARGOYLE

Half-bodies leaning, two versions, one here, one
here. Monstrous order. Varying attempts
to illustrate pure form. One stone
vomits rainwater toward the earth.
The other stone strokes its long beard,
depicting gravity and age
as one gesture. If only
I might crouch next to myself
to see what the differences were.
The horrible array, the mouth
of this statue like a lamprey eel feeding,
the mouth of that statue like an engraved
and vacant line. Not pictured,
a cathedral affixed to each figure, cavity
for a god who goes unrendered,
tho' here amputated for the purposes
of illustration. The engraver, implied.
All other characters
appear as themselves.

HARLEQUIN DUCK

Fat, round-headed creature, as executed
by the engraver in a marshy perch, disguised

by plush pussywillows. The animal
Histrionicus histrionicus, twice named
dramatic, appears subdued and tidy
even with its frightened, beady eye.
One dark stripe across its white breast
like a royal sash. Crowned heads

feed the ducks on their ponds outside
a heartsome city—I love the long grass

blades up their skirts. Little princes
pull painted wooden ducks by a string
around the neck. Victorian parlors
teach small people to hang their dollies;
adults smile in miniature. I am speaking
1/10th the size of normal expression.

Magicians and Harlequin clowns stuff a girl's fear
into a tiny box: so
charming one could take a knife,
carve its picture into a block, and stamp it

in reverse. Look, I'm over-
drawn. I must pay
attention: this

is a duck. A model. Or maybe a Harlequin
decoy: named for Hellequin,

emissary of the devil,
who disguises himself as a doctor
prescribing ridiculous remedies
that would certainly prove fatal if undergone.

MAP

Here Country, here Kingdom,
Boundary: the world
identified. The Sea lies
crosshatched, dark where it meets
little Sea Port Town, marked
by a cross. Oasis at the edge
of Desert and leading away,
Crossroad. Where are you?
the map might ask. Water draws
around Archipelago, or kisses
the Mouth. I am not here,
not in the Bay or Crater,
not Isthmus or Islets.
I may be on Sunken Rock,
labeled among the waves, though
no trace is visible. Soundings
off the shore, the picture
intimates depth; beneath
the image, another idea: drowned
schooners, men's corpses
scattered across the unseen
ocean floor. Once,
a warm hand was here. And
the eyes—I've seen Cliff
and Precipice, striated,
have stood upon Promontory,
beyond which white sun
erases the edge of earth. Yes,
it still looks
like that. Fantastic.

VAMPIRE (TRUE VAMPIRE),
VAMPIRE (FALSE VAMPIRE)

Tilted up, the heads of two bats, jaws
open and fangs parted. False:
large soft ears and a glittering eye.
True: a skull. The dangers are real
and imagined. Portraits of these creatures
come by night and break the skin
of my heart as if piercing fruit.
I dream of winged joys, and their images
fly with me by day. Some moods
flicker in and out of shadow. I must draw
distinctions. Perhaps others
have been bitten, have looked through
dictionary illustrations, searching for
how they dive and disappear. Frightening,
to identify the kinds of intensity,
give them names, examine their shapes.
None of this is to scale.

VISION

A diagram, cross-section
of the eyeball like an onion bulb
and the optic nerve stem
cut off from wherever
it leads. Words
float inside: Fovea, Line
of Regard. Sometimes,
I see only the grey shapes
and lines that drift through
my sight. This isn't how
I regard you, you beyond,
someone please, beyond
me. Each image inverts
itself in the yellow vitreous;
when my heart turns
against itself, I will look
under *h* to understand its apparatus.
The lines and angles go
this way. And the arrow,
pointing out beyond
the picture, to some future,
direction I already
know, even with
my eyes closed:
Fixation Point.

TOBOGGAN SLIDE, WITH TOBOGGANS, & PERSONS IN TOBOGGAN SUITS

A scene on ice as smooth as mirrors—
four persons on a ramp that leans away and out
of the frame: a cozy ride, as demonstrated. Objectivity
does not smile. Perhaps the flying hat-tassels

exhibit joy—though I confess that to be my own
commentary: the couple on the toboggan
is not yet in love, the woman's double-breasted
coat stiffly pulling away from the man sliding with her
and tipping in toward her body's freefall. I believe

the day cold, the sky an unspoken grey elephant.
Discomfort, noun, as defined by feigned gaiety,
a party where the quiet girl does not touch a soul,
she would shatter even under a stranger's fingertip,
and must keep herself tightly inside her toboggan suit,

see Redingote, or Roquelaure, as any of us might see
these words depicted, see Toboggan Slide with Toboggans
and Persons. Buttoned within. And yes, I do read
a small happiness clasped here, something hiding
in her muff, the picture of this. One man on top waits his turn.

VOCAL ORGANS IN VOWEL POSITIONS

Explicit, secret caverns drawn open:
ten open mouths, ten muscled tongues,

their various positions along ten throats.
Behold, the mysterious palate,

and teeth, oesaphagus, pharynx, how
internally they carve sound from air:

Say *all,* say *psalm:*

>The hard palate arches up,
>vault of an unlit cathedral.
>From the moist catacombs below,
>vespers rise, enter the cavity,
>
>then release their notes into the night
>like crows scattering from a belltower.
>I am not afraid to die—sometimes.
>A darkness surrounds the head.

Say *loon,* say *lute:*

>Imagine the lips in a hollow kiss,
>and the hard palate arcs high to buttress
>their softness. My hand curving,
>I've stroked the old hair of a dead man,
>loving him—his mouth vaguely open.
>The diagram does not show this.

Say *eve*, say *plea:*

> The soft palate tenses, wild tongue crouching
> behind a fence of teeth. Antiques press down
> hard; the dead become an imprint. Ferns,
> pondsnails, Darwin, decay, generation.
> The strongest words survive.

Say *boat,* say *home:*

> Wherein the vocal folds, wind.
> Over stippled bone, shade lines like those that mean
>
> airflow: I can see here my open, rushing thoughts
> are not alone. Lo, sound of mind.

Say *man,* say *ask:*

> One can't see the spirit, which is why
> one must study closely the vowel
> where the tongue flattens its wings
> under the uvula. Before vanishing, the engraver
>
> has pressed on me and inked a gothic hope.
>
> I suppose the blank spaces represent light.
> Below the brain, the vertebrae plunge out of sight.

ACKNOWLEDGMENTS

I am indebted to John M. Carrera for his brilliant book, *Pictorial Webster's: A Visual Dictionary of Curiosities*, first published by Carrera's own Quercus Press then in a trade edition by Chronicle Books (2009). The collection constitutes the most imaginative, wild, inscrutable collection of thousands of nineteenth-century wood engravings, almost all of which were created for the Webster's dictionaries. Whether these illustrations were originally meant to clarify or complicate the dictionaries' linguistic definitions of words, one cannot say. In *Pictorial Webster's*, Carrera includes several discourses, of varying wit and academicism, on his project and process; on engraving history, synaptic function, linguistic creation and memory; and on his own quirky and spectacular associative synthesis of select images. If you take this as an inculcation to run out and obtain a copy of his book so that your mind too, at least for a time, might become a whirligig or shining orrery, then you are half correct. I am also truly grateful, not only for the collected engravings, but also for his suggestion that this is, as he calls it, a "sourcebook for creativity." Wandering amongst the images and Carrera's writing as well, the mind becomes double-jointed, triple-jointed, and the best parts of imagination emerge.

Thanks to Becca Barniskis, Sharon Chmielarz, Kath Jesme, MaryJo Thomson, Susan Steger Welsh, Katrina Vandenberg, and Patricia Zontelli for their minds on these and other poems over the many years. Thanks to Rob Edsall and Yolonda Youngs for giving me Carrera's book in the first place. And thanks to Matt Gladue for more than I can say.

OTHER BOOKS FROM TUPELO PRESS

Fasting for Ramadan: Notes from a Spiritual Practice (memoir), Kazim Ali
Circle's Apprentice (poems), Dan Beachy-Quick
The Vital System (poems), CM Burroughs
Stone Lyre: Poems of René Char, translated by Nancy Naomi Carlson
Severance Songs (poems), Joshua Corey
Atlas Hour (poems), Carol Ann Davis
New Cathay: Contemporary Chinese Poetry, edited by Ming Di
Sanderlings (poems), Geri Doran
The Flight Cage (poems), Rebecca Dunham
The Posthumous Affair (novel), James Friel
Nothing Can Make Me Do This (novel), David Huddle
Dancing in Odessa (poems), Ilya Kaminsky
A God in the House: Poets Talk About Faith (interviews),
    edited by Ilya Kaminsky and Katherine Towler
Manoleria (poems), Daniel Khalastchi
domina Un/blued (poems), Ruth Ellen Kocher
Phyla of Joy (poems), Karen An-hwei Lee
Body Thesaurus (poems), Jennifer Militello
Mary & the Giant Mechanism (poems), Mary Molinary
After Urgency (poems), Rusty Morrison
Lucky Fish (poems), Aimee Nezhukumatathil
Long Division (poems), Alan Michael Parker
Ex-Voto (poems), Adélia Prado,
    translated by Ellen Doré Watson
Intimate: An American Family Photo Album (memoir), Paisley Rekdal
Thrill-Bent (novel), Jan Richman
Calendars of Fire (poems), Lee Sharkey
The Perfect Life (essays), Peter Stitt
Swallowing the Sea (essays), Lee Upton
Butch Geography (poems), Stacey Waite
Dogged Hearts (poems), Ellen Doré Watson

See our complete backlist at www.tupelopress.org